W9-ALV-380

HANS HOEFER

Paper Tiger

Paper Tiger
A Dragon's World Limited Imprint
The Bower
High Street
Limpsfield
Surrey RH8 0DY
Great Britain
© Dragon's World Limited 1978
© Hans Hoefer 1978

Distributed by
Phin Ltd
Churchill Road
Cheltenham
Gloucestershire
Great Britain

No part of this book may be reproduced in any form or
by any electronic or mechanical means, including
information storage and retrieval systems, without
permission in writing from Dragon's World Limited,
except by a reviewer who may quote brief passages in
a review.
All rights reserved.

Caution: All images are copyright by Hans Hoefer
or by publishers acknowledged in the text. Their use in
any form without prior written permission from Hans Hoefer
or the appropriate copyright holder is strictly
forbidden.

ISBN 0905895 17 7

GRAFICAS REUNIDAS, S. A.
Av. de Aragón, 56 - Madrid-27
Depósito Legal M 37997 1978

Balinese Stone Sculpture, Art and Architecture

Bali is a small island in the middle of Indonesia, with volcanoes towering over beautiful rice fields, villages sheltering under coconut palms and fruit trees. It is a fantastic land. The Balinese have built upon this a culture of great artistry, one that shows an innate awareness of a harmony between man and nature. Balinese Hinduism gives an overall structure and direction to this way of living, strength derived from centuries-long moulding of Indian, Javanese, and now modern ideas with those of native Bali.

The culture that developed in Bali during the 16th century under King Baturenggong of the Gelgel dynasty is still the living tradition of today. This is the tradition of the shadow puppet theatre *(wayang)* and the *gambuh* dance drama, of the Ramayana and the Mahabharata, or kings and princesses, demons, warriors and clowns.

At the turn of this century, the native arts of Bali mirrored a well-ordered society governed by feudal lords and sustained by the guiding rituals of its religion. The palaces and temples, as political and religious centres of the island, were also centres of the arts. A prince would adorn his pavilions with the most exquisitely carved wood panels, the finest of paintings, and the most elaborate stone carvings and reliefs. His court would be entertained by the shimmering melodies of the gamelan, the soft sways of the classical Legong dance, or a parade of comics enacting a mask play. He would dress in the most lustrous silks and bear a splendid kris with a hilt of gold and precious jewels. Furthermore, as a ruling prince, he was expected to be well versed in the arts himself. He should be able to paint a picture, carve a block of wood or stone, play a musical instrument, dance, and sing in the poetical Kawi language.

Of course, a prince who possessed all of these artistic attributes belonged to the ideal world of superhuman heroes. In reality, if a ruler lacked talent he would support actors, artists and musicians as part of his retinue. Ordinary people, who looked upon their lords as models of conduct, would emulate them by learning the arts of dancing, poetry, music and painting. Thus, art was not exclusive to the aristocracy. Any farmer, merchant, or even a coolie could become as fine an artist as his master.

The opulence of the court — the highest secular institution in the Balinese community — had its religious parallel in the lavish decoration and dances within the temples. Silken materials, gilded umbrellas, statuettes and sacred masks graced the temple shrines during festivals. Throughout the night the temple's orchestra would beat out the rhythms of ceremonial offering dances, shadow plays and dramas of magic.

This convergence of beauty and ritual explains why the arts have endured to such a great extent in Bali. Ritual demanded a continuous renewal of communion with the divine through temple celebrations. The people poured all their artistic talents into preparations for these occasions. New offerings had to be made, new shrines constructed, dances rehearsed, music practised and dramas created. Because of the island's climate and the materials used, frequent renovations were necessary. The only readily available stone was, and still is, soft volcanic stone that crumbles easily and is quickly eroded by rain. This dissolution kept carvers and masons constantly occupied creating new sculptures or retouching the older ones. Artists were called upon to replace cloth paintings that had rotted in the humidity, or woodcarvings which had been eaten away by white ants. Periodically, the island was struck by earthquakes that destroyed hundreds of temples in a matter of hours, causing scores of villages to engage in massive reconstruction.

As artistry was inseparable from courtly life and religious practices, so it was from the everyday experience of the people. The Balinese language has no words for "art" and "artist". Art was never considered a conscious production for its own sake. Rather, it was regarded as a collective obligation to make things beautiful: food exquisitely presented as an offering; a cloth wrap of gold brocade; motion in the pattern of a dance; sound in a musical rhythm. And this was always done with a definite purpose: to create beauty in service to society and religion. A woodcarver carved the pillar of a royal pavilion as his duty to his prince. A sculptor sculpted a stone temple gate as an act of devotion to his faith. Just as an aristocrat demanded the highest standard of work for his palace, so did the people for work in the temples of the revered deities.

While the artist was a respected member of his community, he was not set apart as belonging to an elite. As a "figure-maker" as well as a farmer or merchant, he was called upon when his skills were needed. These he gave freely. He neither signed his name to his work, nor received money for his labour. His prime aim was to serve his community.

In the first decades of this century, when Bali entered a new era as a colony of the Netherlands, Western education, modern technology, and a steady tourist trade opened up a new world for many Balinese. This broadening of outlook was reflected in the arts. For the first time, craftsmen began to treat their work as art for art's sake, experimenting in new styles, themes and media. Some accomplished artists received recognition from abroad, and it was during this time of invention and renewal in the 1930s that many of Bali's finest works of art were produced.

What distinguishes Balinese art today is a fusion of the lively, ornamental folk art — beauty in service — and the recently added element of self-conscious "art". Anyone passing by a temple gate can see that the love of decorative splendour which highlighted the past is still very much alive. As was true in the olden days, the majority of Bali's artists are highly skilled craftsmen who learned their trade by mastering the traditional forms inherited from their fore-fathers. Like so many things in Bali, art is an expression of collective thought. Many paintings, carvings and sculptures are made communally in workshops, where a master craftsman supervises a group of apprentices. However, a small number of outstanding artists who have developed unique styles, their best work often setting the trend for many imitators.

The Balinese artist is intensely aware of his surroundings. He feels his environment as one who is a participant rather than an observer. Local painters, woodcarvers, and sculptors rarely draw from nature; they know nature, and in their art they distill from it an essence which is uniquely Balinese. They scan their experience, select details from it, and give each detail a fresh significance. The Balinese style is an art of particularism. Certain formulas of reality must be adhered to, whether from nature or myth.

A virtue of Balinese art is that it retains its own distinctive character. The people are extremely proud of their creative traditions, yet they are also progressive, and if a new idea catches their fancy they accept it wholeheartedly. Their art has assimilated Javanese, Indian, and Chinese styles into an Indonesian folk art rooted in ancient magic. The relatively new influence of the West will inevitably increase, and with it so will the possibilities and challenges for contemporary art in Bali.

The present art community has two criteria: a work of art is praiseworthy in the eyes of fellow Balinese, or it appeals to the foreign market and is sold. Among Bali's prominent artists who have gained international renown, the two standards of success merge conveniently. But when there is a conflict between them, problems arise which may have a greater impact in the future. A fine artist by Balinese standards may not win the understanding of foreign buyers, and in order to earn a living might sacrifice the quality of his work for commercial reasons. The foreign market sometimes distorts the judgement of the Balinese. Many of the mass-produced half-sized copies of dramatic masks, the conventionally posed nude figures in stone and wood now on sale seem out of character for a people who take pride in superior craftsmanship and attention to detail.

One of the reasons for this lies in the structure of Balinese society. Modern art, created for its own sake, does not have a traditional place and function within the community. The important patronage of Balinese nobles has virtually ceased in the last four decades, and with it, the most influential aesthetic guidance among the Balinese themselves.

● ● ●

In few other places in the world does a traveller encounter such a profusion of decorative carvings, splendid gateways and monumental sculptures as in Bali.

Judging from the multitude of carved temple and palace walls, drum-towers, gates, public baths, shrines and art galleries, it would appear there was an army of carvers scouring the island in search of barren stone. In truth, such lavish adornment is reserved for the public buildings in the villages. Domestic architecture is of little concern to sculptors. The majority of Balinese homes are made simply from bamboo and thatch, or whitewashed brick and tile. Their construction is left to carpenters and thatch-workers, with only sparse decoration carved above the gate or upon the family shrine. Formerly, rajas and lords built glorious palaces (puris) embellished with elaborate carvings and gilded woodwork. Now, as the residences of prominent families, puris remain among the finest examples of Balinese architecture, but they are monuments to an era that has passed. A scultpor today devotes his talents to beautifying private and public buildings of a secular nature (including communal places) and, by far the most important edifice in the community, the place of worship.

Balinese stone carving has a long history. Although no

statues can be dated with certainty to the prehistoric period, the many statues that are sometimes called Polynesian or megalithic have one common factor; they show no sign of Indian influence. This influence arrived, probably by the fifth century A.D., and certainly by the ninth, when the first royal edicts inscribed on stone or bronze appear. There may have been direct contact with India, but a profounder influence came by way of Java: the eighth century Central Java of Borobudur and Prambanan, eleventh century East Java, and the fourteenth century expansion of Majapahit all brought new models, though Balinese ideas of form remained strong. The older statues, those between the eighth and fifteenth centuries, are sufficiently distinctive as to be roughly dated.

Complicating the problem of dating is the atmosphere and surroundings, for in Bali all statues take on a life of their own that makes them ageless. There is something naked in a clean new statue that Bali's moist climate soon takes care of. The stone stains and mosses and fungi grow quickly, for the stone is soft and permeable. Statues seem as old as the land itself, almost disappearing back into it, so thick is the growth around them.

Surprisingly, the origin of the Balinese temple does not stem from Hindu Java, but can be traced to prehistoric megalithic sanctuaries — crude monuments built of large uncut stones which were laid in an open space surrounded by a wall. During the ritual ceremonies of ancient Bali the great nature gods — deities of the sun, of the mountains, and of the sea would descend upon these megaliths when summoned by a priest. Megaliths are the direct forerunners of the shrines found in the inner courtyard of Bali Hindu temples. In some mountain villages that remain ancient customs indigenous to Bali, megaliths are still preserved in the form of stepped pyramids made of rough stones.

Unlike India and Hindu Java, where the temple is a house or a hall, in Bali the temple is a rectangular plot of ground set apart from the profane world by a high stone or mud-brick wall. The enclosed area — a sacred tract of land upon which the deities descend — is just as significant religiously as the buildings and shrines within; this priority is reflected in the architecture of the Balinese temple, in which space is emphasized over mass.

There are many kinds of temples *(pura)*. There are temples for the household, and the family. There are temples associated with rice fields, gardens, hills and seashores. They vary in size from tiny shrines inside hedges or simple mud walls to great temples with many courtyards, scores or even hundreds of shrines, fine carvings and huge stone walls. Each village has its own temples, usually the *pura puseh* or temple of origin, the *pura desa* or village temple, and the *pura dalem,* the so-called death temple. There are also great regional temples, but at the apex of all temples is *pura besakih* on the slopes of the volcano Gunung Agung, the Great Mountain, where all Balinese worship.

All temples save the very smallest have walls and gateways of brick and stone, often elaborately carved. The outer entrance is generally in the form called *candi bentar* or split gate, for if the two halves were brought together they would form a single structure like the temples *(candi)* of old Java. The inner gateway or *kori,* a roofed-over structure, symbolizes the holy mountain, for as one passes through it, it is as if one reaches the summit and the presence of the gods who are believed to reside there. Within the courtyards some shrines are of brick and stone, although most are made of wood and roofed with grass or sugar-palm fibre. The stone bases of posts and parts of the bases of shrines are often carved. Free standing statues are placed on shrines and on either side of gateways.

Although its austere, tapering gateway stands apart from streetside life, the Balinese temple is not a self-contained unit. It encompasses in its design a universal order essential to the religious rites carried out within its enclosures. A temple is always oriented to four cardinal points: the sacred mountains, the sea, the east and the west. The "seats" of the deities are found at the end of the temple nearest the mountains, while the entrance faces toward the ocean. These imperatives explain why temple walls never enclose a circular space.

No special class of architects design the temples. Master sculptors in charge of the construction often take part in the manual labour of building, with the assistance of a number of stone and brick workers. A master sculptor usually inherits his trade from his father. He knows the traditional regulations of building a temple which are derived from a written system of proportions and rules passed down through the ages. All units of measurement are based upon the human body (that of the master sculptor). The temple gate must be so many times as high as the length of his outstretched arms, and so many times as wide as the length of his foot. The front walls must be so many times as long as the gate is high, and so on. Needless to say, no two temples are exactly the same size, but this makes no difference to the Balinese. The beauty of a temple is judged by its proportions and how it harmonizes with the surroundings.

A master sculptor, well practiced in the art of stone-carving, knows by heart the many variations of decorative motifs that form the finishing touches to the walls and gate. Positioned above the entrance should be the figure of *Boma,* a leering monster with outspread hands who catches any brazen evil spirits seeking entry. This, or the ancient swastika symbol, a magic sign of good fortune and prosperity. Odd inventive motifs such as the upper part of a bird's beak or a grotesque face with a single eye are designated to finish each corner. They enclose row upon row of intricately carved volutes, spirals, arabesques, leaves, flowers, vines and tendrils that overshadow the temple façade in a riot of entwined vegetation. The Balinese penchant for gilt and bright colours frequently leaves these carvings boldly accented by strong lines of white paint and blotches of pinks, blues and yellows. They go so far in some parts of West Bali as to coat an entire shrine with brilliant silver chromotone!

Together with overwhelming decoration, each temple has its own personalities: visionary fantastics — giants, devils, sorceresses, serpents and magic birds — that are energetically sculpted in bold postures, as if they were caught in a momentary dance movement, stamping and snorting while flashing their eyes. Their robust bodies and sumptuous costumes reveal the characteristically baroque traits of Balinese art. A temple is never without these awesome portrayals of deities, heroes and magical guardians which stand on either side of the gate. They derive from the imagination unique to this island which conceives the supernatural and divine not as ethereal spirits, but as vigorous super-Balinese.

The gateway and front walls of a *Pura Dalem* (temple of the dead) usually presents a tableau of ceremonial figures such as the witch-queen *Rangda* posed in her conventional stance, or enshrined in an elaborate niche. Yet there also exists a more playful, naturalistic art that enlivens the formality of temple sculpture. One can find in the same temple as Rangda, on the back of the same shrine, a topsy-turvy demon dancing on his hands; a lively figure carved in refreshingly simplified contours, with an ecstatic posture that counterbalances the frozen monumentality of the Rangda.

Formerly, in the absence of art galleries and museums, it was the public buildings, mainly the walls of temples and palaces, that served as display cases for informal, amusing carvings; but these were always given secondary importance to the official statues. One can imagine an old Balinese sculptor, after dutifully carving all the principal statues and motifs, taking delight in finding an inconspicuous corner along the wall where he could freely chisel a miniscule scene of his own fancy. Tucked away at the foot of a stairway, on a pedestal supporting a monumental witch, or behind a small shrine, you can discover the most humorous and suggestive reliefs — vignettes of passionate lovemaking, scenes of gory torments in hell, or such Western-inspired themes as automobile breakdowns, armed robery, beer parties, single-prop airplanes, a blossom-wheeled bicycle, and sinking sailing vessels. Some of the finest examples of this playful secular sculpture are displayed on the veranda of the Denpasar Museum and on temple gates in North Bali.

With the constant renovation of the island's temples, stone carvings of rustic scenes, demons and divinities remain an eclectic showcase for the Balinese spirit reverent and ribald as ever.

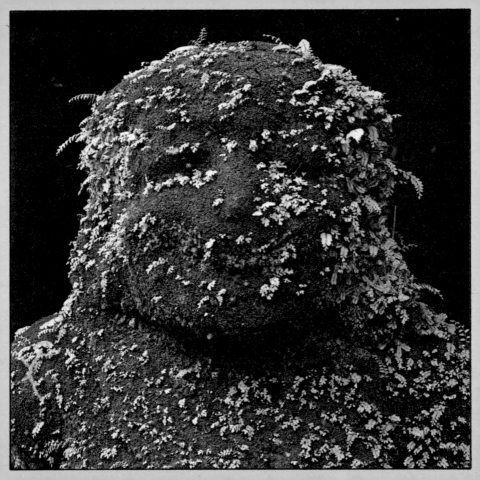